The Awful Grace of God

POETRY BY

Jhon Z Baker

Copyright *Jhon Z Baker*, 2025

All Rights Reserved.

This book is subject to the condition that no part of this book is to be reproduced, transmitted in any form or means, electronic or mechanical, stored in a retrieval system, photocopied, recorded, scanned, or otherwise. Any of these actions require the proper written permission of the author.

To My Wife, Kara Baker, For Support in Spades
My Son, Jackson Grey Baker, For Support in Hearts
And All My Damn Cats, Living or Ash

About the Author

Husband, father, friend, and stranger.

Jhon Z Baker writes poetry as seen through the eyes of a physically disabled schizoaffective bipolar resident of Cook County, Illinois; medicated most days and looking long into the abyss on the others. While not strictly a Luddite, his small studio (room at the rear of the home) contains a typewriter on which most first drafts and many letters are written, in addition to two easels where there is always something drying.

    - ite, inflammate omnia

Contents

About the Author 4
over coffee at a Bennigan's 1
my body feels massive leaning against the headboard at 2am 2
I hid 3
mid-September angst 4
dirt and tar 5
notes on the back of my medical chart written for posterity 6
I think of you oddly 7
the aural ecstasy of accidents 8
this is my star 9
sitting here 10
burned wings of a love letter 11
I'm sorry, I'm not much for words at the moment 12
beginning again 14
Friday to Saturday 16
Advil, opiates, and alcohol 17
so beautiful 18
bites the cheek 19
fly 20
used ideas and worn-out strophes 21
the body capable 23
I've never learned to cope 25
shout into the ether 27
a fatal course 28
miles away and hours to go 29
he wishes 31

swim naked	32
rain	33
HVAC	34
I butterflied her with my tongue	35
dogs by hallow	36
I am grateful to my new anti-depressant	38
bled out	40
chances are	41
square by square	42
the suburban lawn is a patchwork of greens	43
all my friends are drunk	44
my heart	45
after all	46
looking long into the bathroom mirror	47
platonic lovers	48
bitter winter	49
a FB write	50
note from a torn page	51
awake in	52
my cup runneth over	53
backyard	54
the algorithms aren't perfect	55
my feline companion	57
I don't know	58
defacing	59
thinking of Micael	60
how to take a bullet	62

in a bold effort beyond itself	63
I think	64
6/18	65
there are great truths	66
I too can sing the body electric	67
no frills midnight whiskey	68
asleep then not	69
three	70
living with contradictions	71
I am a man of chronic conditions	72
this is a dislocation	73
a scene	74
flowing	75
in memorial- RD (DP)	76
Theo Monk	77
still	78
lens	79
blues and purples #3	80
poem by an abstracted unbeliever	81
wheatfield with crows	82
a friend nearing totality	83
all November 9s	84
better living	85
here	86
as who me is	87
o, Romeo	88
it's a loud world after all	89

eating an apple,	90
these colors	91
on zero street	92
yesterday	93
Chicago	94
surrounded	95
note to self	96
schizoaffective bipolar disorder blues	97
Part 1	97
Part 2	98
Part 3	99
argonaut dreaming	100
sweet hero,	101
all ashes now	102
in the afternoon	103
Bill Evans alone	104
a move	105
darkest Peru	106
in situ	107
on the weight of dryads	108
gone, man, gone	109
journal entry #141	110
moon over the abattoir - a blues	111
Rorschach	112
I fumble yhytoihuyo the barbed wirfeelijhbodojo	113
juggernaut	114
adapt and pose	115

les étoiles	116
waiting room	117
ode to the trash in my neighbor's front lawn	118
schizoaffective bipolar disorder blues II	119
dyscognition	120
the body in pain	121
not what I originally intended	122
song of utility	123
she looks like Rita Hayworth	124
on Whitman's beard	125
without and I	126
new note	127
part one. la tristesse durera toujours	128
part two la douleur durera toujours	129
adds or subtracts	130
sunflowers at lunch	131
from another poem altogether	132
I can no longer dance the two-step	133
these dreams	134
late-night jazz and Johnnie Walker	135
white knuckling	136
disquieting	137
July 12, 2021 - at 6:45 pm	138
in passing	139
3am through the forest	140
phthalo blue	141
to be young	142

clichéd and mediocre	143
$34.00 and a packed suitcase	144
non-haiku	145
90 seconds to midnight	146
ZV2 9190	147
espresso con panna	148
gehenna	149
coffee, black	150
2:46pm	151
I am not Walt Whitman	152
the mean of life is pain	153
rot	154
I mean the whiskey	155
she asks if I'm down	156
memories	157
trepanning	158
maudlin	159
oedipus rex	160
idée fixe	161
sometimes I fucking forget you're gone	162
filcher (without alarm)	163
long way to go (to die)	164
11/9/06 awoken	165
two minutes	166
insomnia	167
making it	168
sol	169

bellow	170
ice pick	171
three-thirty observations	172
euthanasia	173
eat and drink	174
and sometimes bridges look final	175
small things	176
irresistible orbit	177
echt	178
languishing	179
petit larceny	180
disconsolate	181
mercurochrome	182
to the teeth	183
intertwining	184
crooked paths	185
pray for deliverance	186
reflections on broken glass	187
apples and oranges	188
burgers on the grill	189
the short mile	190
reading ahead	191
bitter fruits	192
redacted - blear-eyed wisdom yoked from pain	193
good guy	195
a memory	196
cleaned and godly -	197

K. 361 third movement	198
pain and gravy	199
fair skinned	200
and with and	201
tachycardic	202
take this	203
skrik	204
hiraeth:	205
Brooks Hyers	206
spring in its last	207
sitting on the couch	208
from childhood's dreams	209
covered in case of emergencies	210
do it because it hurts	211
stoplight	212
thus spoke	213
day by day	214
leaving ketamine on the counter	215
self-mutilation	216
Normal, Illinois	218
wounding eternity	219
adrift	220
the world revolves	221
at the forge	222
title: elsewhere	223
mosquito	224
medical breakfast	225

a star	226
haiku #234	227
solitude	228
celestial	229
psychosis	230
by any other name	231
so, dry your eyes	232
a trippy little thing	233
afterlife	234
a brief thought	235
ginsberg makes me want	236
a dying song	237
driving	238
a vast perception	239
space/time	240
flavedo	241
the weather channel	242
a memory	243
Bo	244
a magnitude of life	245
significant implications or subtext allusions	246
anodyne	247
vomeronasal	248
backyard garden	249
a vulpine grin	250
2 lost haiku	251
streetlamp desperation	252

an entropy collapsing ... 254

resolved in earth ... 255

inexplicable gray ... 256

imposter syndrome ... 258

benign ... 259

a birthday greeting ... 260

the morning comes ... 261

yellow ... 262

wandered out of life ... 263

proof of life ... 264

within a gaol ... 265

time rise time fall ... 266

blumensprache ... 268

the discomfiture of youth ... 269

dubito ergo cogito ergo sum ... 270

cosmic crisp ... 271

afternoon assignment ... 272

hope dies last ... 273

a light affair ... 274

repetition kills ... 275

on plane headed to phoenix ... 276

Johnnie Walker ... 277

the wife is worried – ... 278

sunday night brain malfunction ... 282

full moon fifty miles outside Chicago ... 283

plaintive ... 284

the difficult genius ... 285

an elephant of woe	286
Sisyphus	287
relativity	288
ready to go	289
stills in the mountains	290
dry cleaning existentialism	291
words are dry, meaningless	292
road to peace	294
Beethoven's Sonata #9 Op47	296
4:24 am	297
Eurydice	298
I dream of mary shelley	299
late night l'appel du vide	300
I love the children with the dirty faces and uncombed hair	301
edge of the ocean	303
e'ry rose has a thistle	304
king of half sleep and open windows	306
a moment in flight	307
death in granada	308
babeldom	309
I no longer can rely on a friend who once kept me alive	310
mystery	311
after the arrest	312
E.E.	314
excerpt of brotherhood	315
song for K	316
small talk	317

Troy Soriano	318
disambiguation	319
ark	320
part 3	323
a poem redacted, preface – JB	325
a poem - redacted from journal (Semiotics)	328
winter	331
head smashed under bridges	333
eight-pound box of hammers	335
eight-pound box of hammers	337
eight-pound box of hammers	339

over coffee at a Bennigan's

written in a Moleskine notebook

at Bennigan's across from the Chicago Art Institute,

on South Michigan Ave

during a ticketed

art exhibit/ late lunch date

nearly 24 years ago now:

"

I talk

you listen

I talk

you listen

and I curse myself

for talking

    too much

          "

now, married.

    in the kitchen.

and it is

still true

my body feels massive leaning against the headboard at 2am

my body feels massive

dense

made of stone -

each finger a boulder at the end of

    sprawling suburbia cul-de-sac

each by mailboxes representing

        oversized plastic

    monstrosities

we are pneumatic

food and moment processors

under the minor star,

Sol

I hid

bared my soul to the universe

and groped backward at myself

feigned indifference

and

ancient

   solemnity

bred

      debauchery in rose table wine

and cheap

hard-on

back alley

toothless

      blowjobs

or deep in

forests

blankets

      picnics

and poison sumac rashes

to match

mid-September angst

I'm a bit testy today.
think I'll lay down for a bit
or go start a fight.

better have a lie down.

I'm not Walt Whitman-
I never went to war or fought,
 through poetry, for America -

but I do start fights.

and sometimes over a woman-

and so, you see-
I am not Walt Whitman.

dirt and tar

and when

I

die

render my fat into candle wax
and soap

compost this body -

I will phoenix myself
    back
          into
                existence

for

I've never been dead

like I am

now

wanton,
        thrillful,
and exhausted

notes on the back of my medical chart written for posterity

I need to know that the pain ends at some
point. That Vonnegut's sister's last words
are truth.

if I took every pill in my collection
the only thing I could be sure of
is being out of pills
and suffering
more suffering.

the last words were -
"No pain,
    "no pain."

I think of you oddly

I think of you oddly

inappropriately

in moments unprepared for

and gladly

      be well, be happy, find your strophe, under neon lights

      and streetlamps at midnight

me

        (I feel you with words

        undress you in mind

        make love across looks

        and caress with quiet sighs)

the aural ecstasy of accidents

I miss

the

screeching

of tires

    and brakes

        In the moment before impact

    anti-lock braking

ruins the aural aesthetic

    of

    slow-motion faces frozen

looking out windows

    mouth open

and

babies – blue-eyed,

crying

Mama

Mama

Mama

I'm frightened

I'm frightened

postscript: spoken aloud at 90 miles an hour to Siri

who took notes prodigiously

this is my star

this is my star.
      bewildered,
    hanging down
    our heads
this is my star

this is my star,
      vainly wishing and
    wishing on planets
    and suns
this is my star.

on bended knees
with clenching fists
praying or raging at the
Christian God

this is my star,
      to wonder and
    wonder and
    wonder,
this is my star.

sitting here

sitting here

going 66,000 mph

and

it's exhausting

and I'm exhausted

hope is such a terrible thing

hope has such a terrible job

to do

and it's doing it

to

us

burned wings of a love letter

a
star
is
just
the
memory
of
a
star

a memory appearing present and gone

scars
of
half-
remembered
days
and
hope
kindled

like so many photographs over open flame

I'm sorry, I'm not much for words at the moment

but,

I look at you; I
    can plainly see you've aged
some

fewer years than have passed

but your beauty in moments
is still your beauty in
memory
in all moments

and in the next second-

you're gone and left
the shadow of your

intellectual beauty

the beauty of your milky white
  skin, softened
    by looks

the beauty of you

in all

glancing/staring

interested/prying

undressing/covetous

minds

beginning again

The sun is rising again

this morning

in Chicago

once again there was no

discussion

about any of this

I slept

finally

11 hours

five of it fretfully

but

I

didn't have clothes to

wear

or towel to

shower

so,

I went

nowhere

I lay there,

dreaming,

Ephialtes,

thinking through

life's

next

quarrel/

decisions

accusations/

developments or mythos

ends/

beginnings - again

Friday to Saturday

apparently, it is Saturday.

        is it after midnight?

yes.

not by much.

        well, then I love you on Saturday.

I'll always

love

you.

on days called

"today"

I'll always

love

you.

Advil, opiates, and alcohol

my muse has locked herself
      behind bulletproof glass
the genius in the corner is cowering
      and has soiled himself sick

this world is a changeless eternity
and
not everyone was meant for life

"too beautiful"
I hear you say
"too beautiful"
you repeat softly, sadly
"too beautiful"

and
      gone
            gone
                  gone

a very merry Christmas
and a happy New Years to

you
my oldest love

so beautiful

exist faster -
    time
      is
        short
no matter what you believe at seven

and if you fuck it up?

so beautiful,
      or so what.

bites the cheek

a wordless moment

where language fails us

but it comes to me

through me

bites the cheek

to make it bleed

and a rush to journal

document

notations of

sublime momentary malfunction

fly

there's a fly in my bathroom

that has never died

or has

but it's stronger than death

in its swiftness

its smallness

used ideas and worn-out strophes

I am in great

pain

greater than death and less violent

but

equally as final

and

rain pours in

and attracts a sense

of

spiritual cauterization

but

you never know what it's like

to be a Barbie girl

living

in

a

Barbie

world

staring

into a mirror

half gone on New Year's Eve

a tarnished effigy staring back

and

makeup smearing

or gone

from good time

or less so

and

life is a

pigsty

after

all

life is a pigsty

after all

the body capable

I miss the three-day, sport-fucking,
    weekends.
I miss the body capable.

the body that breaks
    further down, toward freedom
        from this constant corporeal pain.
I miss the age where nothing hurt.

I miss the easy word
casually spoken/broken
slipped out over wine and/or
    the death performed in the lap of
    beauty.
I miss the dance of beginnings.

I miss drinks after midnight.
friends now dead or dying
captured in grand revelry on decaying
    polaroid photographs
I miss being caught in positions
      of venerability and chance.

I miss the ignorance of nothing tasting
        as bitter as tears,
swallowed by momentary emotion.
cried silently, alone, or outright
        walking toward red exits
        and yellow taxi cabs

I miss the moment of unrivaled clarity.
    for now, yesterday
        and tomorrow.

but here,
I stand straight.
walk unafraid
    as nothing can hurt more
        than human,
nothing can cut deeper.
deadlier.
sweeter.

I've never learned to cope

        don't know if I want to

I've never learned to grieve

still carrying all my dead

                in the opened

    chasm
of my metaphorical, but life affecting heart

        I was unprepared,
        I guess.   It takes a lifetime
        to get over living
        she said

but

I still grieve life lost-

mine and others-

living now or not
    or whatever

being human

        is the hardest thing

                I've ever done

shout into the ether

this is my bitch,

my complaint,

my shout into the ether

      because

      there is nothing

      today

but

pain.

a fatal course

on a fatal course, crashing

a *fait accompli*

such is life

such it is

so on

and

on

miles away and hours to go

I can see it

when I close my eyes

feel the desert wind

against my face-

the heat wicking moisture from

my bared skin

you drive

toward tomorrow

and the day after

- the wind in your hair

 and your hand surfing the current

 rushing by the open window

open my eyes

and again

alone

in this room

too far away

(dust thrown to the horizon

    from under your tires

    fills the unpeopled

    room

    settling on my running shoes)

he wishes

I love you and I hope you feel closer to whole -

I love you and I hope your heart aches not too much -

I love you in each moment as it passes -

                In each moment as is its future -

I love you with coffee and far away with longing -

I love you across looks and breakfast table glances -

I love you no matter what happens to the heart -

I love you and know that somehow, you love me too -

I love you with sadness, softness, and vibrancy -

I love you and want like every lover wants –

swim naked

I dream of you in red dresses
and nothing.
bridging the gap of venerability
and resolute self-possession.

you swim naked
and wear blue dresses
and bondage
to take the trash out—
escorting beauty onto adolescent
      imaginations
and inspiration to love makers.

I want you happy
or at least not sad -
scarred and redolent,
silken and evocative
a jarring effect on an unexpectant world
shone on by every sun

you are my muse today
and quiet, quiet
a phoenix through your silence
a dancer through your heart

rain

sitting on a couch,
Elgin, Il

listening to heavy rain
and
the birds who brave bad weather

the air is too damp to move
and
causes great pain in my hands and legs

I no longer love the rain

HVAC

I live and die

      by the functionality

      of the heating/cooling vents

except for the odd spring/fall

day/evening

seventy-four degrees

and occasional

summer twilight

with a

cooling

breeze across my self

through rarely open windows

in my lovingly cluttered house

I butterflied her with my tongue

in my dream

you kissed so softly

I lost all breath

les rêves sont des rêves.

mais au moins, dans ces rêves; tu es à moi.

dogs by hallow

the pills I take no longer have personality

white ovals of various sizes
with hard to read numbers
and letters

-

(two white dogs
follow me down the street
and on the bus
where I enjoy the fear
running through the other children
-this is a rapid memory episode
and the
albino malamutes
belong to my childhood neighbor)

-

but I take the pills
and my mood is stabilized
and cholesterol is kept in check
blood pressure kept in check
this one to sleep
this one to keep going

this one to stay the pain of living

and soon I'll likely add

a daily low dose aspirin

(but I miss the dogs)

I am grateful to my new anti-depressant

I am grateful to my new anti-depressant
as finally the thoughts slow after
the old one ceased in proper function

I am grateful to my new anti-depressant
and can smell the flowers as flowers
and the cherry blossoms in bloom

I am grateful to my new anti-depressant
it complements the old and still working
mood stabilizer

I am grateful to my new anti-depressant
and lorazepam which I take at night
to sleep and dream tender nonsense

I am grateful to my new anti-depressant
and the taste of home cooked foods
and the thigh of my wife

I am grateful to my new anti-depressant

and my hands don't shake so

the brush strokes smoothly

I am grateful to my new anti-depressant

bled out

borne out from internalized voices
    from same self-reflection
        and bled out vocally —
(I am glad to live in a time
    where these modern poems
    vicissitudes
    brutalities
    sentimentalities
    could enter my experience)

I am glad to have lived.

chances are

chances are

that

we will not be around to witness

      the end

of

the world.

the party will go on without us -

and

some other, younger generation

will toast

the burning of Earth.

square by square

and I dance a mean two-step

but

slowly

in kitchens too small for tangos

or dishwashers –

on linoleum

through years of age

and small considerations.

the suburban lawn is a patchwork of greens

I used to mow the lawn.

one summer I mowed lawns professionally.
I was young then.

now I watch the lawn grow
in a patchwork of greens and browns.

and that is my involvement
with the lawn.

as involved as that is.

all my friends are drunk

all my friends are drunk
dead
suicidal

or dying

all I'm left with is a box
       of bodies
and broken souls

it's been a hard year

brief periods of disconcerting sobriety
and recovery into madness
my own soul
culled and discarded
like so many shorn chicken bones

and I'm waiting

waiting

my heart

my heart,

larger than life

        and the planets, et al.

is a misfit unto this world

I am the city

I am the city

I am the city

I am the city

the city.

I am that love

I am that broken smile

and bruised aorta.

after all

after all,

crocodiles may indeed be

sensitive souls

looking long into the bathroom mirror

a brush tearing itself through
    my beard
post-nap
post-unrestful dreaming fit

it
pulls at my face, but
I am saved by the narcotics I take

so
I only hear the knots pull out
and a slight tug on my face

my beard, intact, grays more,
but

lives for another half day

platonic lovers

platonic lovers
my chosen brother and sister

death becomes you now

letting go into the ether
and hope for stark odds to be defied

but death knows no master
and this world knows no comfort

so, I persist
drinking whiskey, coffee,
and water-
taking wild chances
with my cholesterol
and dancing
dancing
dancing

bitter winter

winter sits ugly
without her white gown

barren trees in this wetland
ravaged by autumn's deaths

pricks my brain to become a memory
of those who walked unafraid

before
this
scene
became
a
stand-in
for
bitter
loneliness

a FB write

I am cripple

I live a cripple reality.

I am bipolar

I live a bipolar reality.

There are those that say these are not "me"

only things I deal with.

no.

no.

no.

these things are me.

Inextricable.

(I've been there –

on Huntington Beach as the tide rolled in –

naked and alone –

with that far away haunted/haunting look,

that destiny across oceans

thousand-yard stare)

note from a torn page

a brick from my fireplace

has six sides,

as most do.

any of them perfect for

smashing

windows—

if not for being stuck

in the wall -

separating me from

singing birds and

deflowered trees.

awake in

awake in

partial metamorphosis

an incomplete change

but

I stay in bed regardless

of any ability to get up

and

face the day

behind the twenty-first century

plague mask

my cup runneth over

gatherings,

friend sponsored

      but contagious

it's the close proximity of automobiles that I dislike

backyard

a little Bruch to think with

and some hot

    coffee

        in a comically illustrated

            porcelain mug.

it's a hot day -

but I think of you, unencumbered,

    on the bed

and watch you

    as you tend your own thoughts

over your own coffee.

the algorithms aren't perfect

I can't bring myself to kill a fly
but fuck a mosquito

the world is ending
and what should I care
pork chops for dinner
with asparagus or potatoes

all I want:
$40.00
to buy a record.

and earlier —

working a poem
and a stumble in the seventh verse.

I can't be bothered
so,
it ended at six

too many people
out of love
    suffering

in the gutters with wine,

whiskey, and evil eyed

jealousy.

but,

I just can't be bothered

my feline companion

the cat brings me snacks of his taste

in disregard of my own

- little presents to pay the rent

I suppose

in and

out

all day long, but now

having eaten

he lies down—

worn out from the day's enterprises

looking across his kingdom

while the birds call out warnings

to any being who understands

I don't know

morning latte

record shop

long walk

midday shadowless

swamp heat

tall, iced water

medication five times a day

late whiskey

late to bed

another chapter

check phone one more time

another chapter

that's okay—

I don't sleep anyway

defacing

I tear a page from the back of a book

to write an idea

that becomes a poem

and

this

is

the after thought

the minimal effort

thinking of Micael

For MC

make no monument to this body,
let the rivers and roads winding on maps
and fields flowing into one another
from the birds view of a plane
serve as testament.

may there be no wall of remembrance
where people touch hands for famous photographs.
what a landscape of crows couldn't bring into thought
make no admonition,
no stone effigy.

have no moment of whispering
but shout, shout, shout out
your poetry, fill empty halls
and capital domes. dance, alone
or together, naked in halls and alleyways.
ride your full moon lunacy

down one-way streets and secret passageways.

eclipse your broken lifeline,

draw borders onto subway station walls -

trip to New York, Louisiana, Chicago and LA

rip your clothes off in late stage lit drag shows,

ride the rays of the sun.

how to take a bullet

first take your shirt off

and press it into the hole

keep pressure

pressure

pressure

try to remain conscious

and alert

keep pressure

say something stylish

and sacred

you won't have much energy

to accomplish this

and stay alive

but

do it anyway

you

won't

regret

anything

any

more

in a bold effort beyond itself

appropriations
of complete genius
or other-

we pretend

stab at greatness.

stab into blinding winter light
or nearly setting sun.

hoping to draw certain blood
or
at the last

leave a mark.

I think

your

    beauty

        extends

    beyond

space/time

deepened by lines of age

6/18

buried you today

filled my hands with broken earth

and threw it over your body

death being the final blow to brilliance
        and suffering

magnanimity

and your effortless self was always self

without apology

there are great truths

there are great truths to be found everywhere

                and rapacious lies to be found adjacent

but,

you

never

expect

your

photographs

to end

      up

on the

      cover

of

Time

      Magazine

I too can sing the body electric

I write these poems and think
if only they could pay the bills—
and cry,
        but I sing!

the body electric or my own brokenness,
whatever you want!

no matter
there is always more money in
something else
and I am none wiser

no frills midnight whiskey

sorrows

glass

& whiskey

compulsory obligatory

the bedtime rite

asleep then not

3:33am

headache and awake
can't shake either
not enough coffee yesterday
keeping me up now—

no balance in the
evil nature of discovery

three

life is a various separation
        of sordid identifications.
life is a conglomeration of
assorted impersonations.

death is a feel-good retrospective
        of impersonal dogma.
death is a bombastic experience
        of invented nostalgia.

living with contradictions

living with contradictions,

feigning indifference.

I persist.

I am a man of chronic conditions

and if you bless me,

I'll say thanks

wordless at a moment

of deep pain and so many narcotics

my nose rarely bleeds

and I've never bruised easily

this is a dislocation

this is a

dislocation

a skillful assemblage of

et cetera and

et cetera

a cycle of soul drummers

and southern chicken sacrifices at

the front gate of Graceland

a loose impersonation of self

overlooking and

never sighting self

our culture is jazz, blues

and poor elocution

a fragility of coffee house

poets and the war

machine

all

together-colored and successfully

uncollected disaffected ice cream eaters

a scene

or warning
a sprig of truthfulness
and bent knee troubles

I appear calm

my affect is a construction
my facade a conspiracy

I weep in closets and at
    three am

but one mustn't divulge so easily
or a tempest of alarm
will paralyze

not unlike how death
rattles free
our common concerns

or how life lay bare
our unique fears at midnight

or 3 am

flowing

she lay on our bed
— facing the wall

my eyes toward
the line of her body
against light

in all black clothing

her feet bare
and hair flowing

in memorial- RD (DP)

writing from the common well

until the well consumed him

and he became the common source

I loved the man

but never said

and now too late

    I'm told

he knew regardless

Theo Monk

this cat lives in my lap

or seems to when not

    on the table at breakfast

    grokking my indebted existence

still

sifting through the memories of photographs

affecting longing and weeping

      at loss

    and the pangs of faint reminders

of yesterday's platonic lovers and

friends

lens

I thought

I could let you go

    but

        then

  I

        stumbled

blues and purples #3

threat of time, lingers

the opera house trembles
    under weight of voice
        amplified

I hang your paintings

on the stucco wall
    and get lost
        in your strophe

poem by an abstracted unbeliever

nature abhors a vacuum

I abhor the unpunctual

wasted time waiting

for someone,

      something

maybe the rapture

    maybe

          the return

wheatfield with crows

no two people

have ever witnessed

the same

sunset,

          blue

sky,

     or

starry

          night

a friend nearing totality

nearly eight pm
and I wonder how you are
have you eaten today
what did the doctor say

I am slave to these thoughts
and thousands other

all November 9s

on

the fucking

edge

today

teeth breaking

balled fists and bleeding

fuck this motherfucking

plane of existence

better living

swallow handfuls of pills

with cold coffee

it's evening

and the pills

life sustaining

and bitter

here

tired now

11pm

and I try to think of

      the perfect thing

           to say

come back with nothing -

my hands are full of sleep

      and cracks

I try to hold you

but you're falling sand

and my thoughts

   are nude to you

as who me is

reading Allen Ginsberg

contemplating life —

not

as he would often do

but

as I often do

as who me is

as who me am wont to do

o, Romeo

here,

this moment in

space/time

.

a moment of Shakespearian

comedy

clarity

Queen Mab and all that

Mercutian nonsense

I

await

you

      presently

it's a loud world after all

a bathroom fan
makes a lot
    of sound -
so much
  that
It can be heard
from the dining room
    table.

people are always
    full of sound
  and brimmed with pain -
always hearing that from a
   dining room table
even with the newspapers closed

it makes enough sense
for a hardworking
    bathroom fan tho-
it empties a room of steam

eating an apple,

awkwardly dancing to the rhythms of talk radio.

static coming over the line intermixed

with voices interviewing

one another.

it changes as I drive easterly,

toward a days

occupations

and

distraction.

these colors

sordid

dining room associations

and black market broken

watches

poems of this mind

and afterthoughts of thought

screed screened mindless ravings and

dark souls reflected

in windows

backdrop: USA

on zero street

walking—

limping really

with cane in left hand —

    side of the road

kicking up pebbles and dirt

and sometimes shuffling

embarrassed, I eye your breasts

yesterday

  reading

falling asleep

7:18pm

not long day but

  long anyways

nearly Christmas

today the 20th

all gifts simple

and few

  I fall asleep

coffee gets cold

Chicago

overlooking the skyline

across Lake Michigan —

that is not where I am now

dozens of trout lilies

blooming last summer

in backyard —

that is where I am now

surrounded

the angels of pain, descend
        dancing gaieties
impulsive peevish boys
        and girls
innumerable medications tossed
        on sidewalks
streets of tar black
        and devils white
backyard back alley
        black market livings
and the whores of Division
        say their blessings

note to self

I'm exhausted today.
nightmares all night —
        nonsensical.
I take meds for that. no sleep.
today napping is no different.

I'm unwell
are you well?
are you eating?
concern comes from the
        the inner self
        the not-self
the Buddha-self caught in Samsara

schizoaffective bipolar disorder blues

Part 1

Ativan

Depakote

Abilify

Venlafaxine

and the faces fade past the windows

and the young girl fades away

    so I miss her song

and the noise quiets

and the various voices once clear

    now muffled

and I am calmer, less electric

and the colors I see are muted

    the sky less blue

and bridges look only like bridges

    to me now

Part 2

Norco

Gabapentin

Cyclobenzaprine

many times per day

for deep intractable pain

    earned in collision

        that gave me a cane and limp

and my blood pressure!

Lisinopril

and cholesterol!

Atorvastatin

diabetes!

Metformin

Jardiance

and my overproduction

    of stomach acid —

Esomeprazole

and when I can't sleep?

    (nightly)

Trazadol and Diphenhydramine

Part 3

my life is a mess

      of pills and caffeine

my head wasn't screwed on right

      from the factory

they broke the mold

no more of me!

now I'm falling apart

no time to waste

and I'd hate to take issue with

The Rolling Stones, but

time is not on my side.

no, it isn't!

Time is a locomotive heading

Toward a me destination

permanent as I am impermanent

A place where even memories

      of flowers die!

but I do not cower

no

I am not afraid

argonaut dreaming

medications and hard liquor.

these frail stilts holding us above deep oceans.

belletristic notations in lost notebooks.

we are of an army finished by approximation, asphyxiation.

we are fast asleep

and Argonaut dreaming.

sweet hero,

you know
      hope opens the door to hell
    and here I know your mythos
your face or mask
I know your ancient bones
      creak and yearn
I yearn myself in youthful forties
        —redacted—
I creak as well in same forties
but have very little gray
in appearance I've aged fat and graceful
but broken and tired

let's forget the strophes
forget the odes –
    (ancient Greek to teenaged
confessions)
here, I have no place to die
here, only lovers live forever

enlightenment has come

all ashes now

I no longer hear your voice.

not across cafe tables or cups of coffee
or see your sentence or two messages
trying to pull me from my solitude.

you are eternity's ashes
and memory's shadow,
you are the brave only the dead know.

in the afternoon

        it is five o'clock somewhere
rest well
        in ancient throw of bodies

        that at night you might lie awake
rest well
        reclined on bed, loveseat, or chair

        for energy stores like fat
rest well
        there exists suffering greater than death

        tis not nor should be isn't!
rest well
        we violate tender buddha panoramic

        sometimes absurd dreams intonate
rest well
        coffee or cock in hand

        still trying to recover from day
rest well
        feed well - tomorrow we two-step!

Bill Evans alone

scribbling out my schizoaffective disorder

and lonely death

goodnight, Jackson, goodnight

    babe—

Bill Evans on the speakers

and a little more light

    reading —

tho vision is a labyrinth

at the late hour

and the album is set to end

a move

waiting

surveying

so much left to do

they say you never finish unpacking

tho you must finish packing

at some point time must loop backward

and all that was said and done will be unsaid, undone

and chance may favor me again

darkest Peru

the great sadness of death
the despair in solitude or darkness
I don't mind it
here within is my meditation practice
a throwback to childhood —
or meditations on roads of bone
and ashtrays of skull

at now, this point in the continuum
It could be either
but neither

in situ

this beard is my vanity

and breasts my obsession

stretched out on large bed

alone

contemplating old age/illness

    or space/time

preferring nudity but fully dressed

and wearing

       glasses (my other

vanity)

om, ah, ah, om

on the weight of dryads

my soul, indifferent to
    my death
indifferent to the vagaries
    of my existence
indifferent to pajamas,
    slacks, jeans,
        naked or fear of nudity
indifferent of my sex and
    sexual being
my soul,
    light as a dryad
serious as a train wreck

gone, man, gone

gone are the phantasms of youth
and the shadows of youth are gone as well
no longer are we challenged by the
pheromones of hunger but by the pangs
of selfish regret
gone are you, my dear angel, sadness
left here with me
gone your laughter and tears, those here with me also
and this great life lay down on sidewalk
for a moment of rest turned to hours or days

I wish a different existence upon God
I wish a strange defiance upon the middle-aged
a life fraught with desire and unrequited longing
buried in a pine box under the poplar's shade

journal entry #141

I came home and slept lightly.

car travel tires me endlessly

no matter how brief.

but I'm tired again and lightheaded —

unhealthy lunch

and too much fruit for a diabetic

      male in his later forties.

moon over the abattoir - a blues

headed for darkness

hard

as a humanity

shifting landscapes of violence

and sexual expressions

I want science to catch up to the human condition

I want my personal pain to flow out

and out and out

Footnote: talking with

    my imaginary friend

Rorschach

I experience shadows of my dead
in more places than I can account for

muted reminders in spatial reasonings
and prone to fits, sudden tears

burning memories over an open fire
trying to be set free

but what price freedom?
what price mind?

I fumble yhytoihuyo the barbed wirfeelijhbodojo

I fumble through the barbed wire

cutting my thumb

and maybe a fore finger

but I don't gash my hand this time

as that pain I feel

      is radiating from within

for otherwise I am well

still on two feet

and ready

juggernaut

I feel enormous

stretched out to all possibilities

but my hands dirty

gripping nothing tightly

the *enfant terribles* of late-night television

entertain and distract

but there's blood drying

under my fingernails

and I can't stop

adapt and pose

I used to fear the needle

until a crippling gained governance

    over fears

      and I learned

fear is selective

necessity dictates which are convenient

but this is only partially true

or life is defined by loss

and return

or grievance and aggrieved

les étoiles

the stars never wonder what we think

who we are

where we're going

but burn burn burn

some brighter than ours

some more ancient and nearer death

some sprightly and full of spirit

waiting room

a fan running

purportedly to circulate air

but keeps the chill wind living.

Tv with closed captioning

no sound, a

sanitized atmosphere

with cheap carpeting

and uncomfortable single and

double chairs.

I wait by the magazines.

ode to the trash in my neighbor's front lawn

and I look out over the piles of dirt,
broken landscaping stones
a toilet, shattered trampolines,
several disused cars and trailers,
wondering what the hell is my neighbor is thinking.
what in the hell is the grand master idea
that will bring even the discarded beer cans
(by the toilet)
together to form a beautifying landscape.

I console myself by acknowledging the fact
that he's removed the several sheets of decaying plywood
that was leaning against a shared tree.
that were anything to happen in my front yard
out of the ordinary, it would likely be caught by
his cameras and night lights
which keep the front yards adequately illuminated
twenty-four hours a day.

schizoaffective bipolar disorder blues II

reduced to ash -

cinder

blazed out in a moment of unifying glory

like my head was lit by streetlamps

and burned my hair and beard

scorching the skin of my cheeks

and chin

and I was running, running

in the dream, running

screaming, yelling, laughing

in life and detached or detachment

from your position in the round earth

ya know,

people have a lot to say about

lives they've never lived

mine and others

fuck em

dyscognition

it's all I can do

sometimes

to remember

your face

among

the noise

and background

colors

hewn in vivid

blues and greens

the body in pain

a mind undone
the body in pain
staggering
to the next beat
of place in time

pockets full of psychotropics
and several small children

my hands jamming in
several cotton balls
to keep freshness
or the illusion

keys, coffee, cigarettes
and life is different now

the path new

unbridled

un
broken

when everything was beautiful...

not what I originally intended

the windows and doors are open

to admit air -

it's going to rain

she says

 - and so, it does

I curl into a fetal position

wrapped in a blanket

only

to be later awoken

by the chill

of cold

song of utility

psychotic little birds

singing

cacophonous nonsense

as I drive

slowly

by their grove of tulip poplar

and elm

go out!

make love

she looks like Rita Hayworth

everyone's a lover

when

no one

has broken your

nose

and your heart lay out,

unbroken

and

your bones are intact

and

your past leaves your present

unjaded

on Whitman's beard

flowing out to the heavens
with butterflies intertwined -

childless poet-
old soldier,
              what would you think
of your America now?

it was your birthday
and I remembered a photograph
I saw of you, aged 44 -
younger than me now -
you, so much older then,
more ravaged by father death
and that which you had seen –

without and I

I've exhausted this space
this place
this couch I sit upon

words no longer flow
from the fireplace
or the brickwork of the wall

but still, I sit
and yearn from here
with my frail leg crossed
      over its brother

at the ready

new note

a cooling night

no Brood X here,
too north for the screaming
reminder

all I can smell is my beloved's
cigarette smoke
and my four fingers of
whiskey
one foot from my nose

it's
nearing the end of spring

part one.
la tristesse durera toujours

the comedy is over.

those, I imagine, will

be my last words

ached out

on this planet

or the next

part two
la douleur durera toujours

life is a short comedy

with actors miscast

    and sorrowful

our own private hell

clawing up our backs

and resting on our shoulders

adds or subtracts

childhood, from mid-forties,

replete with memories -

I cannot choose which

to harbor on

or delete,

only recalling what,

in the moment,

is forced onto my heart.

the pain and joy

is immeasurable,

like life,

and I cannot suss the ending -

or fix broken watches.

sunflowers at lunch

thank you for the beautiful flowers

they died gracefully in vase

half-submerged in fresh water

on the counter

in my memory

from another poem altogether

I don't know if it adds
or subtracts

a line here or there
beautiful, beauteous
well learned or outsider
doesn't matter
I'm sitting here,
melting with memory
like the tears of an elephant
falling on the African plains

it's hot, hot,
    hot
and I'm melting with memory
altogether alone
in this easy chair
    by the record player
trapped on the African plains
melting

I can no longer dance the two-step

what am I doing here

300 lbs. of muscle and bone

sinew and fat

crippled and lovely, and lazy, and true

I can no longer two-step

or summit small mountains

I can no longer run short distances

seeking out forgotten items

in restaurant booths

I am altogether a different human -

a union of pain, flesh, and

broken glass

look on down, look on down

look on down from the bridge

and weep

these dreams

these dreams keep me distracted

just enough

to stop me from

blowing my brains out

on Michigan Ave

or jump sweetly,

arms spread wide,

off any available bridge.

late-night jazz and Johnnie Walker

what kind of fool am I
to think that there could
    be more to my life than
narcotics, non-rhymed couplets
and creative drought

drinking mixed drinks
        and straight whiskey
chasing sleeplessness away
and tears
men weep
boys cry
and the whole mess ends on
    poignant sadness and
      sometimes the evening news

white knuckling

peripheral movement

voices calling out

some with urgency

some with fear

this is the event horizon

of mental aberration

and it only becomes more real

and horror show

my mind is a horde of misplaced

ephemera

and broken magic

we sing

disquieting

the song of my people -

confessions

contortions

limping along merrily

to unheard rhythm sections.

we dance in our head

our soul, our heart, our religion

coffee for two or

a murder.

the song of my people,

play on!

July 12, 2021 - at 6:45 pm

I stepped onto the precipice

and shook

long nights live on

these long nights

come on

the fall plays its own soft song

and we stumble

remember

the world burns

and watching it burn

we burn

memory will not linger

It's left to become cinder and ash

in passing

the

lost

glance

(and

sometimes

a

broken

nose)

of half remembered

evenings

and old-fashioned ice cream parlors

3am through the forest

howling dogs
reverberate through the stucco walls
through my skull
and I am struck silent

they must have caught a rabbit
it sounds like death
Darwinian echoes
if only for the moment-to-moment slaughter
to return to home and beg scraps
from unwitting owners

better to hear the sound of mortality
than to hear the wounded cry out

Wednesday morning, 3am

and the conversation
dissolves
to a shadow
then nothing

diminished

phthalo blue

the heart is strange

affected

looking out from its cage

under a library of broken memory

misery

we persist,

togethercolored

blue and radiant

togethercolored

together

to be young

popcorn ceiling

shady motel

8:59 and the curtains are drawn

Rush and Division has its hookers

here, I have my wife

low light

her long hair covering her bare breasts

I am naked and newborn

Wisconsin seems such a strange place

to be newborn

clichéd and mediocre

I am a live wire

I am a rock

an island

standing out in an ocean of doubt

a serious lack of compromise

staunch resistance to the

dominant fiction

get out of the path!

one ought to make haste!

poor Yorick!

every cloud and its silver lining

she ghosted me on the boardwalk

bit the bullet

break a leg

call it a day

mediocrity has a way of creeping up

and time marches ever forward

in a relentless pursuit of finality

speaking of the devil

now is not the time to be making enemies

$34.00 and a packed suitcase

Santa Fe, Mexico,
New Orleans,
Boulder,
Anaheim, Tangier, Manhattan

I'll never get these blood stains
off my hands
I'll never get beyond the shores
of Lake Michigan
I'll never again take a new lover
packed and ready
I'll never know this freedom again

non-haiku

the singing cricket
has made a home in my base-
ment. must be lonely

the blooming aster
blazes alive once again
the honey cascades

90 seconds to midnight

abstract time

and we should be drinking decaf

but

we prefer to contest each other

in this ever-menacing scene

our itchy trigger fingers ever closer
        to action

and I wonder if I'll see the flash

or just become silhouette

against the mise-en-scène
        of my phone's backlight

ZV2 9190

there's nothing like
    Zen meditation
    at 90 miles per hour
sitting in the driver's seat
listening to your
    favorite musician
        turned to full
and singing along/ alone
running shoe gripping
    the rubber of the
    accelerator pedal

espresso con panna

drinking my lone coffee for the day

in the quietness of predawn

still morning.

even this ritual comes before my ablutions

or dark intentions

and toxic thinking.

I've fumbled in gait to arrive here

and fumbled in gait to prepare this space

on the porch,

slipper-less,

bare footed.

gehenna

encumbered
crippled
unable to change my oil
or climb trees

I cannot bend to pet a flower
or gallop though the daisies
my gait is shortened and askew

I dream in color
       in physical states
              that cause
                  suffering
       in chronic pain hues

stalked by sudden outbursts
reminders of mortality
I cannot hope to evade
I cannot run to outrun
I cannot kneel at the alter
or unclench my fists
my teeth break
from the tension

coffee, black

out of vices…
last one given up in solidarity
with my wife

and I've enjoyed them all
at one time or another

holding onto coffee's caffeine
as long as I could

but I love the woman
and we've now been forced
by heart attack and blood sugars

we intend her a long life

2:46pm

it's afternoon where I am.
morning behind me.
tomorrow even further -

as I meditate on a spider's brutal elegance
and effortless violence,
there's peace where I am
there's peace

the privileges of being man
the privileges of being human
the privileges of being mad
the privileges of being crippled
the privileges of being father
husband,
brother, son

to be loved
o, to be loved

to know a spider will crush easily under my weight
and to not follow in the performative act

I am not Walt Whitman

I'm a bit testy today.
think I'll lay down for a bit
   or go start a fight.

better have a lie down.
I'm not Walt Whitman-
I never went to war or fought
   through poetry for America
but I do start fights.

and sometimes over a woman-
and you see-
I am not Walt Whitman

the mean of life is pain

it's a bad day
I awoke no differently
Then when I went to bed

I have no nerve left for this life
or at least the zest of it all
I think Kevorkian was righteous

but I don't have a qualifying condition
I still haltingly trip the light fantastic
and limp heavily out to the sunset

decaying green
like a fine patina
on an ancient effigy

rot

took me 18 minutes

to get to the store,

now closed.

tired and bored, waiting -

all the trees on this property are dead

or dying

tailpipe emissions choking

their life support

like auto-erotic asphyxiation

these trees cast out their fate

to winds over tarmac

and their seed

saved in cracks

to be eaten by birds

I mean the whiskey

I could use some whiskey.

a drop or four fingers.

my kingdom, such as it is,

for a glass

and

      maybe

                some

                        ice.

my boots worn out

and emit water

as this soul emits

heartbreak and slaughter.

it's coming on six

and I may go to bed by eight.

this day wasted,

and I take my medicine.

she asks if I'm down

I feel so lost
indulged deeply the
tastes of wine
whiskey
and coffee
I long for unhealthy
trivialities
and rock music

meds ensure
there're no manic states
but fail on depression
and suicidal ideation

fixation

memories

memories deserve better representation

than these poor poems

and heaps of forgotten dreams

the tribulations of this body

in the rancid grip

of depression's distemper

atrocities of thought and heartbreak

a simple gesture

transfixing gaze and breath

a half-moon hangs from our study

of half moons

but only if you believe it

trepanning

the sea aches and yearns
as I ache and yearn
tides ebb and flow
as crime ebbs and flows
and each man's heart
aches and yearns
ebbs and flows

a solitary moon
looking down on us
our broken minds
our breaking hearts

the sea aches and yearns
as I ache and yearn
tides ebb and flow
as crime ebbs and flows
and each man's heart
aches and yearns
ebbs and flows

maudlin

I woke up today
a character in one of those
        English films
or at least I think I woke up

I may yet be dreaming

oedipus rex

today is a conglomeration of short stories

no endings, no beginnings

and poetry is dead!

I've no power

no dreaming

or sitting with psychiatrists

figuring it all out

with Rorschach ink blots

where I see my mother

young

Oedipal complex out of sync

and hyper sexualized image of supple women

lithe and wanting

>	I'm perfectly certifiable
>
>	a dirty old man
>
>	with a crazed mind
>
>	and a fatherly beard

idée fixe

dying flowers are my favorite genus

as death, decay, and living

are intertwined on this coil

and I'm tired

but,

we must recall

that

Macbeth murdered sleep

    and years ago, at that

sometimes I fucking forget you're gone

and I wait for your message
    to come across Facebook
        or messenger
bluntly reminded by my memory
of our last argument
or your beautiful face

so, I write letters that cannot find you
emails that lead to unmonitored in-boxes
and generally, not accept you've gone

filcher (without alarm)

the fly

is not upset

about the

spoiled dinner

wearied

of the strike

by human hands

it

calmly continues to eat

the pilfered rot

long way to go (to die)

- for J.D. Salinger

I miss you

and the tall grass fields
sway with the wind
in an ethereal dance macabre

you were a shooting star
above that field -
I made a wish upon you

when I was twelve, eighteen,
twenty-two, and thirty-three
perennial breathless moments

and now gone
gone
gone

11/9/06 awoken

I feel it.
right this minute.

I always feel it
but
right this minute it is particularly
acute.
memories come back,
pain grips my every fiber -
and I reminisce how
I wandered out of one life
and into another.

two minutes

I am Chopin's Prelude
Op. 28: No. 4 in E minor

each note
a part of my whole
every chord struck
the sinking of my heart
should this moment
only last two minutes
and twenty-one seconds
it will be enough
and I will remain

yours truly,

insomnia

awake

broken by rising sunlight
dancing out the receding moon
these mornings are amazing

and so are you

making it

at times

fifty-dollar whiskey

is the only solution

slight burn to the throat

with barely a grip on

      the heavy glass

just two more

pours of

four fingers

and I'll be there

sol

concrete fingers
heavy chest
each breath a struggle
my heart straining in its cage

this is not a heart attack
but the marrow filling with lead

weighing the body down
till I can only drag my feet
and crawl deliberately toward
the same sun

bellow

wrought iron boot scrapes
do not get me clean
situated beside the doors
      of old buildings
      which I do not enter
but stand outside scraping
for hours or minutes or days

naturally
my boots only get cleaned
from walking through the rain

ice pick

deconstructing my poems

because

they

fail

hoping to reword them into glory

trying

to postpone the killing

of my darlings

and rescue little

resemblances of sanity

I feign respectable

and palm ice into my glass

three-thirty observations

she goes out the front door to stand
      at the end of the porch
watching or waiting
longing or wistful
I've never asked
but always been curious
maybe just fresh air, but
I like the mystery

one of the cats does the same thing

me,
I stay inside the warm house
witnessing

euthanasia

I am going to die
like we all are
and when I wander out
leave my grave close to the bone
that I may escape
give up a last-minute offering
on the altar of silence
and remember deeply

> brother, do you feel
> the worlds sorrows
> brother, do you see
> the world bent in pain
> brother, can you sing
> the healing invocations

yes,

yes,

yes.

eat and drink

these poor days

strewn about

by a resplendent star

I have uncovered the newer

and more dangerous -

the blood thirsty

and ready

but now

worn out, tired

and sporting old prescription

sunglasses

that blur and distort

-to be sure-

these

visions and grandiose

hallucinations

I will merrily dance on -

for tomorrow never comes

for tomorrow

and sometimes bridges look final

outside a darkened room

standing

alone

and waiting
for illumination or egress
no trepidation or pause
but willing

on the precipice
of honor or horror
of separation

It's a precursor

small things

bediviled by
the strange ways
we love
to suffer

sensing a freedom
of lovers
and small things

I know not when the moment came
I know not when the moment's gone
but the impossibility of it
remains sweetest

the small things
gifts of natural order
and the purple prose I offer

irresistible orbit

held in abeyance -
frozen at the moment of
      the little death
I don't know how I got here
but I'm not going home

anymore

echt

living off grapes and wine
whiskey and narcotics

vinyl records and ancient music

slowed by a double bass
electrified
and out of tune
but carrying me towards infinity
towards authentic
and damaged hearts

drink deeply and
stomp your feet

languishing

heavy with pause

drinking in the nights

and early days

sipping the stars

    (now that I've landed

    among them)

far off the mark but comfortable

nearly seven am

and I'm on my third cup of coffee

petit larceny

we write, as you know

we steal, we write

we eviscerate, as you see

spend minutes or many hours

to write! You know

we steal - notes, lines

anything for the final form -

we write,

    or steal

small things

and

petty like Margaret Thatcher

we eviscerate,

as you see

over cups of coffee

and cheerios

for breakfast

disconsolate

I am tired of this Earth.

these people.

being caught up

in the tangle of their lives.

their voices sewn together

in universal cry

"I have nothing to hide

but my loneliness!"

and it's refrain

"love is commodity

and fear of existential emptiness!"

mercurochrome

mercury and bromine

red stained the skin -

lately

water based

and

      less likely to sting the wound

but aged and unused now -

still good for song and poem

still good for something besides

      red stained memories

      and

healing wounds

to the teeth

men are drawn
to smiling women
as lions are drawn
to Christians

it's dangerous to be friendly
       I suppose
it's dangerous to walk the plains
of big cities and twists of small villages
being content and happy
on your own merit
without glances of steel
and
a will to arm

intertwining

a

train horn sounds miles away

    and

she sighs a myriad of stars

       into existence

crooked paths

writing these poems
inspired/
        uninspired
feeding the masses off the apple
taken
        from the tree of knowledge

serious discussions with a snake
about the rapture
religious blather
religious bother
a chain around my ankle
and a nail through my palm

pray for deliverance

baubles of birthdays past

and candlesticks

on the mantle

scenes of murder and pleas

for defense

poetry written in the ear

of the speaker

this carpet is worn and old

these couches are broken

and old

my boots are worn from walking

and I am old and of a damaged heart

and I love a damaged heart

but I am poor, and I feed off dew

scattered on the lawn in the winter

reflections on broken glass

sepia-toned cigarette smoking

and coffee drinking -

scenes from a life's past

dreamt in artists cafes

and street side hustles

over oysters

and

endless breakfasts

apples and oranges

I had an orange
and thought of you
no connection - no
reason

tore away the rind
and
bit
into its softer flesh

burgers on the grill

mid-winter

joyless clearing of snow

I apologize for the brevity of the poem

or the shortness of my mood

I'm hungry

it's 12 degrees

and

I'm sweating

the short mile

red carpeted corridors
leading through twisted paths
beckoning travel and song

trampling
under foot and boot
red carpeted invitations
with love and strength to stand
and
brawl

cool gentle breeze
with face full of sun
in winter -
red carpeted walks
beside empty bramble
over snow
and
broken icicles

reading ahead

it's not

my concern

what you believe

as I

am the one

who does the dying

at least

according to spark

notes

and Shakespearean quills

bitter fruits

metallic mouth sensation
burning the tongue

tastes of acute failure
or raw success

mixed with a bit of orange peel
and bergamot

redacted - blear-eyed wisdom yoked from pain

the quiet banner of determination

full mass and density

gem-like lucidity

large hearted and deep

at some point we surrender

consciousness is taken into the bloodstream

and

disarms through knowing and innocence

a period in the right place

stops the heart,

they will die for it.

violated

as a formed artifact of language

I experience intimates, sojourners

the sinew of shared life

the jungle of old harms, renegotiated

definitive and regenerative

unselfconsciously as breath

we are pinioned

extravagantly sensual

an entrance to another world

good guy

there's a bullet hole in my basement ceiling

and a bullet stuck in the joist

I put it there in a lapse of judgment

- foundationally a moment of terror

frozen in time

that

enrobes me in reconditioned anxiety

it should have been enough

but wasn't

a memory

thinking of you hurts in places
too dark to hide.

it was a beautiful morning -
a beautiful day
a weekend so wonderful
it pains me to dream about -
but dreams are so vivid
and
the colors run

I dare only capture it in words

cleaned and godly -

pain in my heart today
a few hours ago-
chewed two aspirin and proceeded
to lie on the floor.

strange day.

taste of steel and salt-ice
on my tongue
and
fingers.

K. 361 third movement

(Mozart in Vienna)

I have a song in my

heart -

a cliché perhaps

but

rapturous harmonies abound

when a simple oboe comes in

holding an Bb - long

and

eventually a melodious plunge

down the neckline

of a beautiful woman to a

heart shaped locket between

her naked breasts

pain and gravy

the pills make me sick

and

I am sick without the pills

my pain is aggravated without the pills

and

the pills blunt my reactions

so, I take the pills that make me sick

and

go for a lie down

I live because of these,

and

thank God for them

fair skinned

impossible to convert into words
or converge into space/time

you've lifetimes of bursting forth
and
retreating -
your heart, neatly packed away
waiting for the sun
waiting for release
perhaps you're really a hyacinth
about to bloom
and
we've all missed your ultraviolet

and with and

I drank in the moonlight

relishing every swallow

until the night was darkened black

and

I was standing there

with

the memories of each star

glistening around my eyes

and

pouring into the sockets

tachycardic

breaking hearts

are

    for

        lovers.

my damaged heart shows on an EKG

taken at a doctor appointment

and

during cardiologist's examinations

when it was apparent I would survive

I did a furtive dance

and

called my wife

take this

yearning, like a ghost

walking forever through overgrown

paths

brushing by white daisies

and

stepping over

yellow dandelions

I left you with a longing in your heart

and curious wrath in your ocean blue eyes

skrik

I wake up the same person

stranger yet still

watching the sunrise on a shattered mirror

and

hear the red rooster

howl

starting another day

I feel a sympathetic scream welling within

but

quell the necessity -

I am no red rooster

I am no shattered
                        sunrise

hiraeth:

I know of no better word than this.

I am foolish with self -
whiling it away
whiling away this tearful effigy

hiraeth,
a meaning closer to heart than
imagined television memories
mistaken for life

Brooks Hyers

here, my assurance drop away -
I lose all direction
as though lost in Gray Gardens
where
chirping birds hide away in unruly
arborvitaes.

    I wander through,
hopeless
under the watchful eyes of Little Edie -
a parody of affectations
and
fear —

spring in its last

this affect will one day stop our hearts
and
nothing on earth can prevent it

more coffee for two
over baguette and scone
a chilled morning
on the back three season porch

the cats run around
and
climb their towers
the chair is broken but functional
for now,
it matters most the drinking
and
non-verbal communications

sitting on the couch

cool breeze moving from window

to window

no crickets chirp in my house

in situ, listening to birds unafraid

of the cat - they're new to the yard

I think

the screen door doesn't latch

it moves open and closed with the will

of internal air pressures

and

vacuum

the squeak of the hinges

are no more musical than stepping

on a spider

from childhood's dreams

I hear the words:
no one had the childhood they wanted

and so, I ask my son
to whom I have given my
everything
and
everyday

and he doesn't know at 18
what he'll wish at 45

covered in case of emergencies

I'm ambivalent about Jesus,
but saved the life of a daring rabbit
on Good Friday
it may have been the Buddha
     or Christ reimagined—

it careened out from the grassy section
of one curb toward another.
In line with my tires -
with no one behind me I hit the brakes
and saved it in its stupidity.
now -
it owes me a life debt like so many
squirrels and
cats

do it because it hurts

beside you
sitting here
standing here
dancing here

cavorting wildly
waiting solemnly
walking quietly

    -    beside you
naked from birth
patiently abstracted
invisibly pained
I am beside you
look for me

stoplight

well

    well

well well

we glance into our scrying mirror

bravely

and

as we rise, my love

I am beside you

and we dance

our sacred dance

in kitchens and bedrooms

knowing the adoration of two

and

the tastes of twenty-four years

thus spoke

the Christian God has no name
and there is no tombstone to be found
but,
      by generations,
                He is dead.

I've been mourning for thirty years
a palliative mourning
easing the sense of gradual disappearance

a man once said aloud in a wood
"God is dead"
and I say so quietly in waiting rooms
and cafes
knowing unbelief
and the breaking of a heart

day by day

I'm sick of these

pills

and the need to take them

I'm sick of these 15-year-old

chronic pains

and

schizoaffective bipolar 1 disorder

I'm sick of these insane

selfsame demands

and long periods of discontent

(in winter or otherwise)

today I feel aimless

tomorrow I'll feel shame

leaving ketamine on the counter

- for AJF

heavy tired

watching Tv with the light off

noise on

strain to hear over tintinnabulation

    in my ears

the hours zero in

and close

the recliner is good to me

and

the coffee is never good enough

self-mutilation

unbearable sadness and deep
intertwining ecstasy
I live on in spite of my self
creating
refining
and throwing away my occupations
for we are wretched
without
and I cannot stand analog time

peaceful aggravations
momentary distractions
and colors so vivid it blinds

hand held up to my face
where do the angels go?
what do the dead know of?
how do we cope again?
five stages and complete recovery
every day, every week, and every month
physical detachment
or painful subjugations
of self and those others who
feign concern

maybe unconcerned or puzzled

in concern

blue light pops but vision fades

and everybody still goes "Ahhhhh!"

Normal, Illinois

Hampton Inn
and there's no bible
    in the nightstand drawer
so, I read Kurt Vonnegut
    as a superior replacement

the pool is warmed but I stay in my room
reading, thinking, not sleeping
though the meds are tiring
and the bed small

the blanket provided
fails to cover my feet no matter
how I rend and pull and twist
bodily contortions until a semi-comfortable
position is achieved

the night is long
without Gideon to guide
and my thoughts are lost
to the movie theater like darkness

wounding eternity

my life
is
silk
     shadow
and I look
for
where
     to bury
the time I've killed -

a genuine moment
or a path to eternity
a train locomotive
and
the nightly news

adrift

no life raft.

no magic pills.
no swaddling words.
no panacea.

the match will not ignite.

we put away the candles,
away from the window,

compound our concern
into deep wounds

and

starry night.

the world revolves

on particular axis'

we hide in our wounds
visceral, deep, and haunting
self-inflicted and togethercolored
brought on by white knuckled
tenderness

we hide in our hearts, hardened
by god
our neatly designed fortresses
penetrated by pain's fragility
and
radically exposed

we walk back toward immortality
passing death and its phantoms
where I'm ugly
and
unguarded
pitifully unwritten

at the forge

a beautiful place
where time and heat blacken
hands
but I leave, hands clean

a tourist through their experience
on a threshold between the now
and the after - looking
across the Mississippi

large bridges
on the verge of collapse
or in stasis for eternity
a flux moment

I have my silver for the ferry
and Charon will pilot the ride

title: elsewhere

I don't write much

when it rains

especially

when it rains like this

torrential downpours

calling for a blues

and humidity covering

the windows in a haze

stuck now

inside

but where would I go?

Mexico City

or escape to southern France

just in time for winter

mosquito

I haven't killed a thing
since the first or second summer
      in this house
it is
however
not a bloodless home

our nearly all black cat
has killed hundreds and
catches birds
only to break their singing necks

I suppose
mosquitoes should count
as I smash them out of
existence

or whatever
existence
a mosquito has

medical breakfast

my medications aren't vogue
no Xanax, Adderall, or
Viagra
maybe Valium still registers high
among the housewives
but I don't imbibe.

I am known to take narcotics
- this for chronic pain
and those are always popular
but I no longer drool on myself
with fistfuls
as it all attempts
to drown the pain

I could easily become
an alcoholic
and
I've been there before
attempts at a barfly
and well sauced by 3 pm
but insurance doesn't cover
that particular medication

a star

constellations of memories

blip in and out of existence

even these thoughts evanesce

until life is beautiful

and never hurts

but

this -

a great lie

from an unreliable narrator

haiku #234

late summer rains
beat out familiar rhythms
on a shingled roof

solitude

I will not live another 100 years

nor fifty

an ephemeral vision in the night

orphaned thought sweet to taste

stone to hold

and

hungry

celestial

my eyes punctuating the sky

little bullet holes of light

      shining through

and blood as rain soaking the ground

around my running shoes

all the poetry of Korea

comes south

the 38th parallel

psychosis

hearing birds chirp at 10pm
and questioning voices drawing nearer

a screaming tinnitus

I long to sleep through this cacophony
I long to dream of large women
I long to sleep the day off
but I cannot
I cannot close my eyes through the veil
I cannot cope with memoryless windows

by any other name

bullets blow petals off roses

shrinking the beauty to the stamen

thistles still puncture

and cut

from preciousness to brutal

      thug

does it still smell so sweet

dried, dead, or blown to stem?

so, dry your eyes

what horrors have these mirrors
seen and collected
these mirrors now broken
      and seeping dreams
or terror

the movements of a home
the things echoed inside halls
unseen, unheard
and
walls do not talk
      or hear for the plaster
      and packed R-19 insulation

if walls could talk
we would threaten
but,
they cannot and
mirrors know - so we break them
with fists and bottles
      ready at hand.

a trippy little thing

out of character

out of time

out of place

from time out of mind

to shared space

the two lovers

forget and run

kiss and depart

labeled for mass

distribution labeled

for the breaking

of hearts

afterlife

so, trapped by the words of ancients

by the severity of a mountain lion

by our promises intended to keep

    and broken

        like the heads of biblical children

        dashed against rocks by holy men

it's apropos of nothing

a heartbreaking approach of apathy

or death

the wishing away this list of ordinary life

a brief thought

leaves freshly
        fallen
into wind blown
        communities

my cat steps curiously

Ginsberg makes me want

Lucien Stryk makes me happy.
Plath does not but makes me want.
Whitman pours into me.
Bukowski makes me want to read Bukowski.

H.D. makes me want to read Keats.
Sexton turns me on.
mainly now I want to go to bed or
make more coffee or make love.

Kerouac makes me want to go go go
like roman candles exploding on a wave of
east coast jazz and Charlie Parker.

Berryman makes me want to sleep
and dream of Ego and Id.

Cummings and WCW blur in my mind and
all I can think of is a red wheelbarrow,
and blue umbrellas to remind.

a dying song

a lonely cricket

lost in the wood shop and

singing plaintively

painfully against the night

and

no one picks up the phone

at two am

driving

the world unfolds itself

a little at a time

making clear lamp lit corners

and shadows of the unseen

unregistered

      unregulated

previously clouded skies

      become crystal

and ash

a vast perception

on one side of the scale
I cast a giant shadow across the earth
blocking the sun's sky
I press my weight against the moon, stars
on the other end I am a firefly
trapped in a jar

I find my letters strewn across your desk
torn into and read voraciously
a compliment I believe

I am here -

you are there -

we are
        where we are

I am a firefly trapped in a jar
a sun pressing against the sky
a moon lying in a bed of stars

space/time

the fourth dimension

available,

      unattainable

the sun rises and sets

everyday

expectantly the same

like watches wound properly

or

time stretching out

in front of our shortening lives

a measure linear

continuity of a single direction

until you unwind

and your history becomes unknown

flavedo

I bite into the orange rind

and am colored in instant

      bitter regret

too motionless to peel the fruit

but not beyond importance of flavor

easier to let it roll off my fingertips

onto the table in

excruciating slow motion detail

the weather channel

78 degrees today,
sunny
        according to the forecast -
anyway

I will continue to believe this -
not looking out the window

now, if only there was a way
to shut out the sounds
of pouring rain
        thunder,
lightning

a memory

reading poetry off paper napkins-

art drawn in black ink and smudged-

coffee regular filling chipped porcelain mugs on cracked saucers-

the seriousness of my youth

captured in 24-hour restaurant windows

contrasted by the humor of my middle age-

open menus spread on lunch counters-

sugar dusted spoons lain peacefully

on ancient linoleum trimmed in aluminum

and worn through from years of sanitized cotton rags and friction-

waitress chewing gum to stay awake-

loose bracelets jingle 'round her wrists-

she always remembered my name-

2am then-

2am now-

Bo

I miss my mother-in-law's cat
strangely more
      than I miss most people -
(the people who've gone before others
the people who the pacific has forgotten)

It is not incumbent upon me
to eulogize the names of all my dead
here
(with compassion or otherwise
in teary eyed repose or otherwise)

I do so miss a few of them tho-
bright spots in a chaotic landscape
each buried in a pauper's box
(forgotten by friends and time
while I exist on the other side of space)

a magnitude of life

between a rock and
a hard place
and I'm just fucking flabbergasted

in youth,
a magnitude of life from this moment
        backward

quarreling with impulses star crossed -
        opposing
obligations forming decisions
    I could not claim
but tethered to

when I didn't vanish, but returned-
I felt the call of the void
forever steering and seducing
bewitching
enchanting a disenchanted life

significant implications or subtext allusions

maybe I'll go the way of Van Gogh
or Emily Dickinson

for now, at least
I know I'll not legacy as a great poet
    or spiritual advisor

the beautiful dance of chaos
the quarrel of life, loneliness, and madness

call it eternity

anodyne

this is life

this is vagaries and

        balderdash

it really is boring most of the time

 - as Berryman espoused

before he looked over that bridge

and never thought better of it

vomeronasal

men's bathrooms located in seedy places
      where so called alpha males congregate

put away that cheap gas station
Spanish Fly
once found in the condom dispensing
vending machines-
humans can't smell pheromones
      bought and applied, or
        naturally made

to be specific —
we don't have an adequately
functional Vomeronasal organ
(look that up)

we use our eyes - not our nose,
in most cases anyway

but keep buying the prophylactics
    from the scratched white
      quarter condom machine
   or local pharmacy
as we can't wear blinders and still see

backyard garden

once again
I have not witnessed
the flight of
an Ivory Billed Woodpecker

they,
long considered extinct,
do not haunt my hollow

but,
I remain hopeful
about an appearance
on one of my white or red oaks
teeming with food
or peeking out from a hole
drilled out on the side of my
white and green garden shed
that was
painted by my wife

but not for the woodpecker population
it was an esthetic choice

a vulpine grin

a voice from the ether
substantial and delicate
      as angelic dictionaries-
(this needed at exactly 1:22am)
arrived
a beckoning, heeded and lovely

a controlled self-annihilation
and we are gone gone
gone
used up tho not wantonly

(most so-called wizened fathers
suffer others with their rosy retrospection -
the vague offerings of corporeal worlds)

2 lost haiku

late summer leaves
I wonder who
   my child is

stepping over fallen leaves
and dismantled watches
making sure not to stumble

streetlamp desperation

I wish I could see the stars
from the foot of my driveway
where it meets the end of the road
while the rubber soles of my shoes
grip the asphalt like rare earth -

light pollution stretches far
      from Chicago-
corner streetlamps only help
      when disabled
      or otherwise lying adjacent
      to the curb

Cepheus
Ursa Major and Minor
stunningly
crisp were this blacked out

a human's eye
    deep field in desert conditions
        that do not exist here
save a massive power failure
or overactive imagination

then

ennui rises suddenly

I've grown
        accustomed
to the shallow breath

and

have only the synapses

of casual drug addiction

and

painful memories

to make this dispossession significant

 - a lifetime of developed regret
      and alienation
           forces an aspect
I'm criminally underprepared for

an entropy collapsing

out of place, time.
a certain ennui of homesicknesses,
a sudden hushed realization

I've never been home -

but

I can't tell you this without
causing harm.
without,
breaking your heart.

resolved in earth

unmoored and directionless

a cliché perhaps

but

passionless,

drowning in heavy rain -

I never learned; you know -

to swim

in community pools,

ethereal waters, or into the tides

inexplicable gray

1.

forced contrition is a null proposition

dreamers, lovers, and artists
all depart the same way -
absent
the moment after empyreal breath

2.

 - in dream - or dread -
a moment passed or period

    -

was she waving? or drowning?

am I in a coma feeling the night spiders
crawl on my eyelids and forearms?
hearing the confessions of nurses?

fear gripped from sudden, and insofar
unexplained, mother and child death

3.

I don't mean sorry as penitence

but still as a sorrow of circumstance

and plight

conditioned upon straightjackets and

the padded walls of uneasy grace

imposter syndrome

I am the great pretender
half filled
half abused notebooks -
the inspira,
A little daemon crouching in the corner
a genius in the Greek sense
still, feigning dilemma
Illusory philippic

I am the base of my worst fears
coffee, iced water,
whiskey neat is the breakfast of champions

I kicked the end table
and bled for two hours

there is no up from here

benign

the unmistakable sound of chainsaws
against living and dying wood

early morning -
faces in the window, and
the house is shaking
unnervingly so -

expatriation of the rot
through fungus and scorched earth policy

a birthday greeting

may the earth offer you enough

may the sun shine warmly on your face

may every breath be deep and full

may you fall among the stars

may you dance joyously

may you drink deeply and love fully

ad astra per aspera

ite, inflammate omnia!

the morning comes

the morning comes

and too quickly

I'm left with no quality of sleep -

it's an old complaint.

I sleep in waves, no sleep, then sleep,

bizarre nighttimedreaming in between

my mother texts and I am fully awakened

      by the sound of grating smartphone notifications.

new furniture in a new place

and

the indifferent stars above

if I should survive this

It would cause a pain

for which the dying

have no time to heel

yellow

at fifty miles an hour it occurred to me

the interior scent of the automobile

bore a strong resemblance to dandelions.

at 65 I was sure,

I could see the buttery yellow

float between my pupil and the windscreen

and I felt the vehicle push harder into night

recalling the few summer days spent in fields

stretching out on heavenly long grass

I closed my eyes and tears swept down my cheeks

the contrasted heat of tears against the air conditioning

of the Ford SUV set to high kept me aware

wandered out of life

I know this darker place
the precipice of night
      and light and half-light

I live there in waking hours
and in no hours
caressing the railing
leaning, staring with abyssal longing

crying out, weeping
unnoticed and
electrified

these are the stretched hours

headlong into aching blue light
or bright light
or the end of light

proof of life

all wounds found in mirrors
are antemortem markers of history

unwritten and/or willingly forgotten
passed along by oral tradition
or paintings hanging
in adorned hallways

newspapers in cafés
never carry
the poetry of a disabused heart

within a gaol

hope.

I wish no such prescription

for myself

my tenderness

for naught

and I sit,

hyperaware of my melancholy

With an aspect scattered

      into the wind

life is enough with its majestic tragedy

time rise time fall

I cannot help the cracks formed in my body

light passes in and out

discordant reverberations

give way to syllables

clearly heard

repressed and smothered to tears

 - ashen

I am separated

your beauty lingers in my eyes

as Chopin lingers in my ears

we are being swallowed whole

rendered into candle wax

to light the way for one another

you are the secret hero

    -   my soul possessed

a twin star dancing eternally

ready to super nova and

consume my entirety

POSTSCRIPT:

I'm beholden to you

and do not possess the proper word to say it

I'll be your brother through all eternity

and we'll chase each other through all of time.

blumensprache

1.
blackened
with ash and rain

burnt toothpicks
standing in the median

old friendships forgotten
like lost lovers

peri-apocalyptic
books, warnings, and erotica

2.
the iris means "you fill my heart,
only to plunge it in darkness"

but really, it's
the purple hyacinth

your friendship eases the torment
of my misfortunes

thank you, beautiful
perhaps I offer, oleander

the discomfiture of youth

time spent waiting is interminable

stuck in a stretched moment of pain

you do nothing

frozen

as you weep

more silently than nighttime

at nine years old

in your bed

in a shared room

too afraid to wake the others

dubito ergo cogito ergo sum

our humanness

our humanity

is determined

by checking a particular box

on a screen of blank spaces

like Virgil to Dante -

the only way out is through

midazolam

vecuronium bromide

potassium chloride

cosmic crisp

the soft glow of your phone
on the bed as you sleep next to me

(I catch it as I return from eating an apple
at one in the morning)

It illuminates nothing of you
only underside the pillow
that you slumber upon
the underside of the pillow
that softens your dreams
the underside of the pillow
you use to partially disguise your eyes

afternoon assignment

mourning the death of
    a stranger
buried alone, in a pine cuboid
with
fistfuls of earth cast down
rattling the hallow carved for
    this pauper's occasion
even the officiant's eyes cast far away
      along the horizon to dinner
      and day's rest

hope dies last

I come and go
        through others' lives

seemingly without notice

half deaf
in pain
and mentally aberrant

Death has my face folded in his wallet

he's waiting with cut string
and faded timepieces
with the night so long
and dawn still further away

moments contemplate themselves
and dust arises to speak

I never want to be human again

a light affair

a light lilting noise -

a smallish cacophony

most often in my left ear

sometimes your snore is more cute

than intrusive

it barely punctuates the darkness

of a cinema

or late movies

enjoyed on the couch

with or without air-popped

buttered popcorn

repetition kills

literal or not we bled on pages
        and pages (and pages) of uncertain poetry.

to draw the necessary inks
men need wounding
and bleed by action
women bleed with efficiency
and pain borne onto them

and

dying roses are not broken promises
        as are crumbling petals no longer red.

on plane headed to phoenix

draw no maps on my body

from the air there are no

state lines or divisions

this is how it is

how I am

my self has no divisions

no maps

no way of existing

only being

sand leads into water

water into rivers

rivers into dirt

no thought

just does

& the clouds are always

changing

metamorphosing

Johnnie Walker

sitting now with my favorite four fingers
        neat in a rocks glass
and lamenting an inability to wrap around myself
to cause my brain to release oxytocin
and calm my over-reaction to negative stimuli

a mind bred for anxiety, delusion, disordered thinking
and…
we're dramatic by design -

I speak well - it's an illusion
a fool for everyone -

        to dissemble - to pretend I'm a John Keats
or a John Berryman
a Donne, Gray, or Dryden -
to get away with the world shifted
and faces without eyes

and
faces in the windows
a phantasmagoria of waking experiences

a carefully curated museum of appearance
and affect

the wife is worried –

- for Dan

(a little sentimental drivel
in the opening of
the second movement)

I am a sentry
for our collective heartbreak

I've been careful

I've not been this inebriated
in greater than a vicennium
and the last in forgotten bars of angels

it's the
secrets, you know.

the
medications, you know.

two bottles, you know.

I held it together with white knuckle intensity

a white-knuckle sobriety

a white-knuckle stability

but my confidants know a different me

a stain on new growth flesh

and new brain synapses

new brain cerebrovascular incident

and fresh heartbreak

over new lines and forgotten strophes

and you,

this love to you - this damaged and broken purple prose to you

this endless sadness in invincible summer

to you —

whether you accept or withdraw

whether I've wounded myself

        in your knowledge or presence

trying to grip

a shattering narrative with elusive control

whether I've wounded you without knowledge

or not

but

broken hearts know no further atonement

- which is grace

the brokenhearted know the taste of iron
        on their teeth and wine-stained lips
- which is grace
today I know the relative smoothness of
        1200 ml of whiskey
        in glass after glass
        and cubes of ice
        melted away -
which is grace

you:
salt of the earth, hero of these poems
you are not ostentatious by any regard
you are not gauche
to you I apologize for the fragility of my nature
the unique patchwork of a *sui generis*
a blinding color discernment of this natural
world
and know our place bravely

now finally:
naming is a kind of violence
an unconscious nomenclature
used to strip wonder of its humanity
unadorned beauty
but

I don't traffic in tragedy

broken chainsaws

or felled trees

Sunday night brain malfunction

I always wonder if a
random
      abstract
    poem
is going to awaken a sleeper agent
who will kill everyone at the poetry reading

so, I don't write like de Kooning painted
but do my best Matisse

full moon fifty miles outside Chicago

72° heavy winds from the south –
standing under the starry'd night sky
and this is what I'm thinking…

así va la vida

plaintive

the plaintive long
wail of a house cat

upon seeing a forlorn enemy
through the glass door

and he cries his voice gone
over one tortured summer

the other never made a sound

the difficult genius

fragments of sleep
like so many tricycles laid out
late on Christmas Eve

I've never skipped a hag stone across ponds
or
tried any smoother stone adjacent the Chicago River
never peered through the worn hole for my destiny
or broke round rocks looking for amethyst

in dream and in life a warm friend guides me
"the 10-inch square tiles are asbestos"
I'm told
and walls are rotted plaster with breaking lath

2.

I often dream of post apocalypse migrations
caring for children with the dirty faces

I've never needed the evidence
of a rising sun
but for the warmth on my upturned face
and the bending of flowers

an elephant of woe

trapped in an atmospheric haze
filled with gadflies
biting and blocking reflections
from the pool

there were no horses
and
if there were
they would be bucking,
kicking at the nothingness
of vanished delicate inspirations
in the meanwhile of
summer cookouts
filled with
the trite conversation pleasantries

Sisyphus

narcotics and whisky

that's

the many gods ambrosia

a sip of ethereal madness

and it seems

that

certain kings push

boulders up eternal hills

or sleep under hanging swords

but

rest is only for the wicked

and murderous

relativity

time,

unobserved,

can be any time

, but once observed

becomes not enough

ready to go

while
I write these small poems half asleep
and slightly dreaming

type with eyes closed
at times because I cannot bear to open them
at times
with hands outward
toward the iridescence of heat
and blinded

well,
the day is hot,
humid
and dripping —

and we long for rain

stills in the mountains

reaching for water

in place on my nightstand

but grabbing yesterday's moonshine

to be shocked back into consciousness

lying in bed thinking:

goddamn if she isn't beautiful

and we're both undercover

away from the hue and cry

apart from

this world drowned in avarice,

sadness,

    and grief.

dry cleaning existentialism

the clothes returned to me

from the low cost

somewhat effective

dry cleaner adjacent the

      corporate pharmacy

all the destiny and fate washed away

and a medium starch

a burnt sun reaching out for borealis

looking north and up

twilight

and buttoning the shirt

to the collar –

words are dry, meaningless

words are dry,
expression faceless.
the ladybugs came here to die
on my window -
baking in the sun.

a hundred portraits
unhung,
composing city life.

walks along South Michigan
in Chicago -
children think I am homeless
and dirty.

find Buddha in the patrons.
find Buddha in the hall.
find Buddha on the front steps
of MOMA.
je suis beau!
find Buddha in me!

on these steps I ask for a light -
and I am

not thinking that I'm going to write this

a year later, or more, sitting at

my desk.

where

ladybugs come to die on my window.

road to peace

I am sorry, or perhaps not
but
I don't strive for peace
to be had for humanity
nor foisted upon it

so many write it on signs
and stand on street corners
selling vain hope instead of
methamphetamines
some make a solid career of it

peace -
not only impossible to achieve
but not truly desirable either
boring
tho oft promised
and oft dealt in by the slick
with slogans, hats, and long marches

"peace now, it you want it" -
you'd be crazy to turn it away

but I turn it away

out of hand

and having heard many arguments for

I find none are persuasive

none are positioned to last

none grant peace without subjugation

each tire laboriously

only maintaining uneasy peace for certain peoples

never without the lash or unwilling bondage

Beethoven's Sonata #9 Op47

- for Dan

I apologize for the fragility of my nature

for
within me I have no endless winter
or invincible summer
within me there is a teeming entropy
and at times
the breaking of shoelaces
      at four in the morning

we, you and I, defy augury -
evil portents in the eyes of judgement

we live or die together
by look, nod, or glance
the blade is brandished
and blood stains the dance floor

4:24 am

and I hear the birdsong from
a species unidentifiable to me -
happily calling out, in rough measure
for love? games of the heart, or maybe
just bird fucking after wine
and cheese

so
sing! call out! but know
my beloved cat stays out -
sport hunting for blood
fighting over ideas of territory

but you, birds, cannot hide your nature
for safety
nor want to - you warble sweet tunes
with no thought of death
like a crooner in afterhours clubs
astride pianos with tip jars
marked for oblivion by contract

but
I don't traffic in tragedy
this is merely the entropy of suburban living

Eurydice

   - for K

I have loved you for lifetimes
and lifetimes
more I can offer you

I am in love with you,
        catastrophically so
we've rended apart our own existence
        to become one
when apart,
weep to the heavens
and bring sorrow as rain

there is no apart,
as there is no measure

there is no glancing back

I dream of Mary Shelley

I study the journals

and notebooks of doctor

Victor Frankenstein

attempting

to replicate -

(on a smaller scale)

the grand theory

through application —

a vain attempt to apply such balances

of science and imaginations

for the restoration of a life

altered in late 2006

late night l'appel du vide

two and twenty-four past midnight

I aim

to phoenix myself out of despair,

brokenness

and

chronic conditions -

to propel grief and rage

past or period

to roll

backward through auguries

and wander through this life

for I've tried having faith

and paid away all innocence

but Death, my only friend,

and I chase toward eternity

with no recognizable legacy

or dream

I love the children with the dirty faces and uncombed hair

I was that child, with uncombed hair
playing amongst the other children.
I was that child, reaching up to touch
the oddities, being pushed away by older brothers.

I was that child, who stares at my adult hirsute, smiling face
and is unsure.
I was that child, being pulled away by a hurried woman, a
tired mother, yelling out and wanting to play more.

I was that child with the pigtails bouncing up and down
in countermotion to her shoulders.
I was that child, with the dirty face sipping the cola
greedily, with pocketful of toys and secret playthings.

I was that child, lonely in the corner with no one to lead
or follow, no one to hold hands.
I was that child, yelling louder and bolder at each win -
fisting against the air the losses but playing again.

I was that child, there, holding daddy's hand and
lightly crying, there, racing to the bathrooms, there,
asking for ever more quarters, there, eating the cheap burgers

and fries dipped in torn open ketchup packets
looking and wondering.

I am that child,
with the dirty face and uncombed hair.
I am that child
with pigtails bouncing in countermotion
I am that child
lonely in the corner
I am that child
holding daddy's hand
and
wondering

wondering

edge of the ocean

on

the fucking edge today

teeth breaking

balled fists and bleeding

fuck this motherfucking

plane of existence

And here I am

on

the edge of a bridge

overlooking

    the

ocean

momentary serenity

e'ry rose has a thistle

I've been pricked by every thistle I've kissed

every rose that had a touch

to my face

or fingers softly bled

on every penned note

for

a

now

forgotten

lover

or

unrequited moment

recalled disparately in dream

or

in passing,

the

lost

glance

and a

broken

nose

of half-remembered
evenings

and old-fashioned ice cream parlors

king of half sleep and open windows

not a man, but
a boy. perhaps
next to open windows where
birds come to sing, where
wind & breeze come to play -
in loose curtains where moon
lies gently tickling the arms
of youth and kissing the forehead
of prayer

here, the faces of clocks tell no hour.
here, our eyes & lips have no looks.
here, the silence of childhood exists.
here, those cloths are at your feet
and my dreams

a moment in flight

October 25th
and we celebrate the birth
of John Berryman.
heavy with the burden
of his smashed skull
and dream songs.

his final entry,
a comment left
on the Washington Avenue bridge
in Minneapolis, Minnesota.

death in Granada

I'll be 48 in a brief moment,
for a brief moment

Lorca was younger by a decade
for a brief moment

Berryman, the better part of a
decade further

all
spent under moon and stars

all men of haunted haunting measure
 - the racking moments
that
wile away from fingertip
to fingertip

lines of poetry, gasoline,
and ash –

babeldom

   babeldom   babeldom
           babeldom

at the sound of crumbling daisies
and cacophony of voices crying out
    in voluminous language

I can hear breath
      not seen since February
or March
each synapse a sound, a TV playing
      a different channel
an alien dialect

a babeldom reaching to God

I no longer can rely on a friend who once kept me alive

- to L.M.S.

(estoy triste porque mi
vida ha sido dolorosa)

we are no longer friends
because I could not ask for
strength you did not have.

mystery

why should mystery give its last
name?

every death where I fall deathless
is denial of truth, beauty, and
sainthood

we are all saints upon deliverance

the God of Death is forgiveness
and ease
no pain
all so easy to speak
after
      the
            ephemeral
                    passage
                          on Styx
and Acheron

it's all so easy to say
lowering into the earth
the last endless night you'll
ever have to master

after the arrest

lovingly drown in
        the black, drunken
      waters of Lethe

I see children as small gods

the bravest of warriors

2.
It's all so easy
until
    after
        the
            arrest
until after the accident

now I'm a hard man,
a difficult case
a triumph of will
through certain disaster and
waltzing away

the docs keep telling me
I shouldn't be alive

I shouldn't be walking

I shouldn't be bitter

I should be glad
        to be functioning

vita brevis
        vita brevis

vita brevis

E.E.

Cummings wrote some wonderful stuff
about the professionals of southern France.

painting them wonderfully decadent
all in lowercase affectations.

in absorbingly beautiful lines
like a soft tear running up a sheer hose,

he wrote shaken, he was deeply smitten.
and likely incorrigible,

carrying her heart with him
whatever was his, was writ by her hand

excerpt of brotherhood

a woundless kinship bearing scars
from the brokenness of our inimical lives
we bare down on our teeth
steel our grips against slings
      of fortune and arrow

speak well of me, brother
be not gauche in remembrance
or tearful in confession
remember me not for worse days
and imagine me no hero in my grave

hey,
we must think of Sisyphus as content
we must believe in a pain free Prometheus
we'll be no hungry ghost buried in layers of hell
but finally confess to our personal Guido
finally confess to one another as priest
finally feel no burden or emptiness

loneliness melted away like so many chocolate Jesus's

song for K

I love you in lost light

in darkness I love you more

in the corner of low light

or no light

in the morning

it's beautiful and you glow

I love you from this

to no end and quiet on the couch

I love you resting in bed

and your long touch across

looks and time

and I love you

and I love you

and I love you

and the fires that burn within you

small talk

small talk is a gathering of lies
    socially acceptable and required

her elegantly lined face -
eloquent
    with
grief -
she stood as
the abominable beauty of our time
admonishing each suitor
as tho they were riddled
with childhood misconceptions
and dirt under their fingernails

Warhol would've been in love
Basquiat was
in the final moment of each
neither knew she had been
and back
and back again

Troy Soriano

I'm sorry for my arrogance and spite.

I can't believe it has been seven years -
the wound still fresh.

now you have the answers
we debated over with no regard
and
callous,
you've had seven years to parse them -
seven years to anatomize -

let's meet at our coffee shop
and you can tell me everything,
again.

disambiguation

Wednesday morning 3:21

she had committed harakiri
laying out on the floor with a packaging knife

her daughter had found her at about 3:21
in the morning

it was Wednesday
harakiri, on the floor, packaging knife
Emily home at three

not reading the morning paper
not letting the dog out
not spending another winter in Chicago
not thinking, not hurting
not cleaning the floor
not percolating coffee
not cooking breakfast
for Emily
anymore.

ark

I wanted to build an ark,
so I built an ark.
I wanted to sail across oceans,
so I sailed across oceans.

I sailed to my death
but failed to die.
broken
in pain
a fine madness
with the world colored beautiful
and sky an unfailing blue.

I left the city.

left behind Clarke and Belmont homeless
polishing leather walking
boots.
I left being lit by streetlamps
sitting in corners
under flat light of desperation.
left the window washers
tattoo parlors
left the cafes where young boys,
old boys laugh easily with homosexual motive.

left traffic, redlight, abandoned buildings
art houses, dance studios, opium dens
unlit coffee joints, bright coffee chains.
huddled, dark under evening porticoes
seeking out soporific dope;
a prodigious blindness.

2.

drunk on red wine or whiskey;
memories illuminated or fabricated
in winter where crocuses have no bloom
and life under the crushing weight
of foreign language operas
arias
elegant gibberish.

and so in love
beyond years or measure
youth or less.

belletristic notions
left in black notebooks
filled with variations
of you
as subject or apparition
in white dress
silken veil
with shoes off.

the under currents of sex
and whispered echoes of joy
with pornographic limp.

a Spanish tango.

3.

it's all faded jazz,
blue paintings.
innumerable waves lapping the hull.
bow pushing out, cutting
untraceable patterns, pathways
away from the city, suburban landscapes,

rural forgottens and flowered forget-me-nots.
a miasmic noise,
a constant playing, discombobulated
music on old vinyl.

vibrant, beatific –
and sky, cerulean,
wisps of sundrenched rain clouds,
formless platitudes,

scenes from childhood
filmed in dream sequence
a moment rewound, rewound
played forward, backward, inestimable.
sweet, sad trumpet, an instrument of my childhood,
sings effortlessly, mellifluously
Sketches from Spain
gentle sweep of the sails and calm seas
with the world colored beautiful
vibrant, beatific
and sky an unfailing blue.

part 3

mercy.

mercy.

the good girls gave in
to *enfant terribles* of late night
        sophistication, movie drive-ins -
Caligulas of teenaged heterosexual addiction
homosexual a priori instinct.

ultramarine blues playing in back-room wasteland
tones, color, emotions of form.
she sips brandy and smokes cigars
        a Cognac dipped haze, muted consideration
sandpaper verses of strange fruit in sequined dresses.

we are the drunkards of brass rail barfly joints -
we celebrate half broken neon signs.
we are the soulful moth occupying
        the half-light of fading streetlamps.

we are the desperate, misconceived.
we've shirts off in a moment of frenzy
and misaligned allusions to greatness
we are the bop Shambala meditations

      of time-space inequity.
and I cannot free you this,
heal you this.

but I am with you,
in a body beautiful,
shattered, crying out
on back porches, smoking, singing,
dancing you with crazed two-step and Spanish tango.
protean tongues lapping at the innocence of milk,
slingshot flames and firecracker wisdom
twisting our bodies around images
      and starry night scenes
          on freshly made beds too small for comfort.

sheathing my pen in high fidelity smiles,
we weep like soft-skulled school children
 - aesthetes of playground bike rack bloody noses.

a poem redacted, preface – JB

- for John Berryman

startled by impact

cumulative

a hunger for youth

he was fifty

J had seemed much older

as though

absorbed and consumed

in the very intensity

of his memory.

a matter of life

       and death.

his ambition propelled

a

striking photograph in Life magazine

it would be eleven years.

his amours

turmoil

consumption of alcohol

alchemized

to represent the agon

essential attributes

syntax

tone

diction

cadenzas on carefully

tuned strings

allusion

meter

primal manifestations

to be difficult, "obscure"

obscene.

a besetting consideration

narrative accounts

or

the world seen through inebriation

dreams

a disjointed film

shapes

presences

identities

sometimes in mid-sentence

often presumption

singular

voice and vision

effeminate

intimated, elusive

wild,

unbearably beautiful.

a poem - redacted from journal (Semiotics)

love made him jump
suddenly

Eden, the fall and
return

turn now, to the
challenges
with variations of astonishing

strength

in an elegiac sense
the skull is smiling –

> his mother watching
> silhouetted poise and
> valor
> a metaphor of liberation

condensed
pause, he
gets up and walks

away.
"these fucking beautiful boys
drive me crazy"
impotent
potentially dangerous –
a kind of saint from the otherworld

this kid has serious problems

breakfast in the room and we
finally fall asleep.
too fucking perfect.
even when you die
birds are singing –
L.A. L.A. L.A.

he left his mark everywhere

woke up late
under close observation
loose
intuitive
almost comical
his position quite clear

leaving the show

xxxxxxxxxxxxxxxxxxxx

the sun was just going down

"beautiful."

winter

late night, the
mail did not arrive
on a Saturday.

limping hard with
stars to walk home under.

stop under streetlamp,
the house dark
under such starry sky.
beautiful.

beautiful.

making prints leading
off into brightest winter sun.
come morning and
no memory
of being out,
no memory of
starry skies or
decades of
nighttimedreaming.

all memory now papers

and papers

and cars passing at

65 miles per hour.

head smashed under bridges

I am little more than an idiot.

ringing meditation bells and lighting a candle for reasons I no longer comprehend.

I do not read playboy for the articles or look at the painted nudes for inspiration.

there is a catalogue of cunts and scripted pornographic dear editor letters.

and so most magazines read on a third-grade level.

I want a photographic memory.

I am not more than a human excrement machine – a shit factory,

with piles of words from page-a-days that I've not bothered to memorize.

listening to piano sonatas, Chopin, though it is always Beethoven.

there are no birds outside where Dunhill Internationals burn in chill wind.

and it always comes in with white noise and muffled voices.

if I told a snake to feed you, would you eat?

2.

I am soft.

fatted on candy and motionless hobbies and professions,

lifting the weight of coffee and flint lighters

- sex and masturbation are the extent of exertion.

looking out the window to suburban melting snow landscape,

images of children playing in sixty-year- old neighborhood

that is yet to be incorporated.

3.

it is a fixed game for me

my heart will explode

young and tender at 53

they will look

but they will not find

my head smashed \under bridges

above rivers

on rocks or concrete superhighways.

eight-pound box of hammers

- the first part

the cold comes in fits
      and starts
winter will set in overnight
and tomorrow will be tucked in white
and spinning tires

watching through a frosting window
and feeling it grip my shattered legs
      this is a forge of pain
      chronic in its mastery

this is where I could love you
a sharpened thought
searing in dreams
      searing in wakeful consciousness
a curse only your hands could ameliorate
and do

this is where I could love you
wounded and crying out
baring the scars the prove my mettle
the scars 'round my heart

down my arms and legs

carefully hidden by black uniform

and ever intricate tattoos

all to cover the many lives I'd like to forget

eight-pound box of hammers

- the second part

my problems are small
        inconsequential
or
life threatening and often
menacing

doubtful admonitory realizations
obscure my crowded mind
-

standing naked in the master bath
I note that I age in photographs
not the bathroom mirror
and that saints come from places
no saint would dare tread

sainted life
is a precipice of staggering
        proportions
to a being smaller
than an inch
in stature and girth
but

I've two mother figures that pray

a mother who prays to Archangel Michael

and a mother who prays to Jesus

that I might find freedom from my doubt

and freedom from an unending pain

      that sleeps, wakes, walks,

          and lays with me

pain is the master of all domains

and death is the release

there, it is and was,

the thought to weep

and weep and weep.

eight-pound box of hammers

- the final part

grief is the phantom pain
of a severed life
of unrealized potential.
grief is the price paid
for having loved –

and as the fine details and subtle scents
of each faded connection dissipate away
or renders reinvented and proximal

I bask in what dreams came true
        not the sudden departure
that was brought
        to a planet unaware
but made the worse for it

but we know that
Betelgeuse is still a collapsing star

www.ingramcontent.com/pod-product-compliance
Lightning Source LLC
Chambersburg PA
CBHW071951070526
44583CB00015B/1147